YOUR GOD?

YOUR GOD?

Léon Joseph Cardinal Suenens

A Crossroad Book
THE SEABURY PRESS / NEW YORK

1978
The Seabury Press
815 Second Avenue
New York, N.Y. 10017

Printed in the United States of America

Library of Congress Catalog Card Number: 78-60877
ISBN: 0-8164-2192-7

CONTENTS

FOREWORD

In February 1977 the Sheldonian Theatre in Oxford was filled with members of the university who came to hear the Primate of Belgium, Cardinal Suenens expounding some central themes of the Christian faith. The directness and courageous cheerfulness of the Cardinal's spirituality were at once apparent to all his hearers.

With this book, his addresses are sent out to a wider audience to whom they will be as warmly welcome as they were to their original hearers at Oxford.

Henry Chadwick

Christ Church,
Oxford

1

THE GLORY OF GOD

*Introductory: 'If you believe,
You will see the Glory of God'*

O Lord, before speaking to these your friends assembled here, I would ask you to be present yourself. You say that where two or three are gathered together in your name, you are in their midst. Lord, be here! I do not want to speak in my own poor, human words. Lord, speak yourself. You are the Word of life. You alone can speak words of life. Speak yourself, O Lord. Let me disappear. Let your voice be heard. Amen.

———————

Thank you, my dear Bishop. Thank you, all my dear friends who have come here tonight. It is a privilege and a joy for a Cardinal, now growing old, to share with you some thoughts on what God means in his life. For you are the world and the Church of the future—and I see in you a wonderful future.

I was glad that the title of the Mission, 'Your God?' is followed by an interrogation mark. I saw it as an invitation to be personal—to tell you something of my own experience of the Lord, if I may so put it. It is difficult to speak in a personal way. But it won't be personal all the time. Don't be afraid!

Nevertheless, I feel a kind of challenge to tell

you, very simply, what it means to me to experience God as my Father, the Son of God as my Brother, the Holy Spirit as the breath of my life.

The hope which is in you
Also, the question being put in this way, we remain true to the tradition of the Apostles. When Peter wrote to his disciples he said: 'Be ready at any moment of your life to give testimony of the hope which is in you.' By this he means, 'Don't resort to learned arguments, sophisticated philosophy, theology and the like. Just be ready to testify as to why you are a man of hope.'

It is very simple, really. I try to be a man of faith—and hope is nothing other than faith looking to the future. Yes, that is hope. I shall try to follow in the steps of John the Evangelist who says:

'That which was from the beginning, which we have heard, which we have seen with our eyes, which we have looked upon and touched with our hands concerning the Word of Life, it is of this we will tell. This Life was made visible; we have seen it; and, by our testimony, what we have seen and heard, we declare to you, so that together we may share a common life, in order that the joy of us all may be *full*.'*

* I John 1 v 4.

I shall try to follow the example of Peter and John.

———

Before reflecting on the Christian of today and the renewal of Christianity, I want to look with you briefly at the situation in our world.

Claire obscure

In painting a picture you can use bright colours. Equally you can use dark colours—make use of shadows. If you look at the world today you can paint a picture in the style of Rembrandt, *claire obscure;* 'light and shadow'. You can emphasise all that is going wrong but, no less, the many signs there are of hope.

To give an idea of today's world with its darkness and its light, I want to read to you the opening passage of *A Tale of Two Cities,* where Charles Dickens describes the world as it was just before the French Revolution. I read it the other day and copied it out for you as being totally relevant to our epoch. Here it is:

'It was the best of times. It was the worst of times. It was the age of wisdom. It was the age of foolishness. It was the epoch of belief. It was the epoch of incredulity. It was the season of light. It was the season of darkness. It was the spring of hope. It was the winter of despair.'

I think we can say that today, no less than yesterday, it will depend largely on each one of you whether the world will be a world of hope and light or a world of despair and darkness. And if we look, not at the world but at the Church, we can use almost the same words. The history of the Church down the ages has been summarised in a striking passage:

'It was incredibly sad how low the Church sank on occasions and how high it rose at other times. The peaks and the valleys succeeded each other through the long centuries and there was never a time when it was all peak or all valley. Saints lived in the worst of times and great sinners in the best of times.'*

If we feel dissatisfied with the century in which we live, the only thing to do is, I think, to put a question to ourselves—to say: We are living in the twentieth century, nearly the twenty-first. But suppose we lived in the sixteenth century? No, I would not like that. The seventeenth century? The eleventh? The sixth? The second? No. All in all, I think we must be grateful to be alive at the present time.

Something is changing.
And now I want to look at the new situation

* *Origins.* N.C. Documentary Service, May 1973, p.712

in which Christians find themselves.

I say 'new situation' because something is changing, something has already changed. What is happening in all the Christian Churches is, I think, that more and more the young of today (and it is likely to be the same tomorrow) are no longer Christians simply because it is a family tradition to be Christian.

Young men and women are less and less disposed to follow in the tradition of their mothers and fathers, or in that of their country. There is a reaction against tradition. The young, unhappily, are not interested in the past. I hope that is not true of Oxford. If here in Oxford you're not interested in the past ... well, I don't know what to say!

But, generally speaking, the young are not interested in the past, only in the future. Only the future has credibility for them. The past, they feel, has been responsible for so many evils. Young people do not want to pursue a course just because it is a tradition. They want to pursue it only if they have made a choice freely, committed themselves of their own volition.

We have many baptised persons. Baptised, yes, but are they Christians? The world is filled with baptised non-Christians, and this creates a new situation. It is no longer realistic to expect that a Christianity handed down to us will be acceptable—it must be a Christianity of choice.

And that creates a problem.

Baptism

However, I do not think we need change anything as far as baptism, confirmation, and the other sacraments are concerned. The baptism of children should continue. I believe in the Church's tradition in the matter of infant baptism—it is essential this should continue.

A new commitment

But we need to introduce, in all the Churches, at an appropriate time and place, at a specific moment, some form of 'catechumenate'* or initiation—a new commitment to Jesus Christ as a living person, with all that this entails in our daily life.

It is very important that we should realise we are baptised. But are we consciously Christians? We have to face this, and devise for future generations an occasion at which our sacramental baptism is affirmed afresh.

Something, indeed, of this sort should be introduced in the pastoral life of the Church. For example, this present Mission in the University could be, for some of you, a wonderful opportunity to view afresh the choice made by your

* Instruction or initiation into the fundamental Truths of Christianity.

father and mother on your behalf at baptism—to reassess as adults, in the full awareness of maturity, the precise nature of that commitment. Yes, something of the sort should be introduced in the pastoral life of the Church.

How it began

Consider how Christianity began. It began when the Apostles came out of the Upper Room in Jerusalem at Pentecost. It began when Peter proclaimed that Jesus had risen from the dead. And when he had ended his first 'sermon,' they asked him: 'what shall we do?' And Peter answered: 'Repent. Be baptised in the name of Jesus. Then you will receive the gift of the Holy Spirit.'

Repent! This implies conversion, renunciation. Repent! Be baptised! This means entering the mystery of the death, life, and resurrection of Jesus and of yourself, in the fulness of the Spirit. Something should be done on those same lines.

In the very early Church baptised persons were adults, and so it was natural that at the beginning those instructed in the faith should be adults. There was a considerable period (as much as two or three years) of instruction, prayer, penance—this, supported by the community—before the day of baptism. When Christianity came to be publicly acknowledged, children were, of course, baptised in the faith of the father and the mother, which was right and proper.

Nevertheless the direct confrontation between the individual and Jesus Christ was lost: the choice, the commitment did not take place in the same way. We should try to restore the original encounter with Christ as experienced by those first converts.

It is important that we should hand on faith to the future generation by our testimony and that, for the young, their experience of Christ should be a personal reality. We need a new type of Christian people.

Are we Christians?

Jimmy Carter, the President of the United States, said on a public occasion that he read one day of a sermon that was to be preached on the theme: 'If you were to be accused in court of being a Christian, would you be found guilty?' It made him think.

We should all think. We should ask ourselves: 'Are we really Christians?' The trouble about Christians, it has been objected, is that they are NOT Christians. The solution is obvious. It is to be what we profess to be—CHRISTIANS. And this involves a revolution.

We can no longer, I repeat, be Christians because our neighbourhood is Christian or in consequence of our past. To be a Christian means making a personal decision on one's own responsibility. And to do this is supremely important in view of our new situation.

We are to hold in Rome, in October, a synod* of Bishops. Two hundred bishops representing the entire Church will assemble for a month. The topic will be catechesis† for young people. I have asked the Holy Father to include the topic of a neo-catechumenate‡ for more mature persons—already baptised and confirmed. I hope this will be possible in one way or another, for here lies the problem.

It is not just a question of giving lectures, having talks, holding conferences: it is a question of having the support of living Christian communities and preparing a renewal of Christianity in an atmosphere of prayer, fasting, and mutual support, so that finally as a result a new kind of Christian generation may emerge.

It is at critical times in the history of the Church that we need to do something of this kind. Ignatius of Loyola introduced his *Spiritual Exercises* as a Retreat of four weeks, which was nothing other than a means of Christianising Christians.

* Synod: A representative assembly of bishops convened by the Pope.

† Catechesis: instruction in religious belief:

‡ Neo-catechumenate: renewed instruction in religious belief at a more mature stage of development.

No one reproaches us for being Christians. I have never heard anyone doing so. But we often hear the criticism that we are not Christian enough—not Christianised enough.

And so on this wonderful occasion offered to us here, we should pray about this—pause for a moment to pray and to ask ourselves what it is the Lord wants to tell us, how he wants us to be touched by him.

A renewed creature

I would like to consider with you some conditions which should be implemented if we sincerely wish to be renewed Christians both today and tomorrow; if we really wish to renew our Christian vitality. If we want to encounter God, the living God of our faith, we need simply to become a new creature. A new creation. Paul speaks about the need for this new creation. The need to be reborn.

I would ask you to remember the conversation between Jesus and Nicodemus. We have to be reborn, renewed—but reborn in such a way that the Lord uses the words 'renewed creature'; reborn, like a child in the womb of the mother. This is the first condition, if we truly wish to find again, in its fulness, our Christian identity.

But this first condition is a negative one. We have to disappear, if we are to be reborn. We have to enter into the mystery of death, which is nothing other than the mystery of baptism—and this means our being plunged into the death of Jesus and, through death, attaining resurrection. We have to renew ourselves spiritually, just as baptism renewed us sacramentally. We have to die to ourselves, otherwise there is no hope of a renewed Christianity.

We have to empty ourselves of ourselves. We need a vacuum. It is not possible to fill a vessel that is already full. Something must be emptied: otherwise the grace of God cannot enter, cannot work. We have to lose ourselves so as to surrender to another. We have to surrender to God. And nobody knows what God will do if we surrender to him.

Now, if this is to be taken seriously, it means we have to disappear, give place to Jesus. 'I do not live, Christ lives in me.' And if we follow to the end the logic of our faith, we have to confess that there is only one Christian: Jesus Christ, and that we are Christians in the measure in which we allow him to live his life through you and through me. That is Christianity. Another takes over.

Depossession of self

Christianity is a mystery of 'depossession' of self. And this emptying is a pre-condition if we are to be filled by the Lord. Once we know and accept this, then the Lord can become alive in us. This is the first condition. You can call it by different names; you can call it humility—essential, fundamental humility.

Before coming here I was reading a poet whom I much admire, T.S. Eliot, when I came upon the lines:

'The only wisdom we can hope to acquire
Is the wisdom of humility. Humility is endless.'

Yes, if we disappear, if we leave a void, there is room within us for Jesus Christ. Now this means we really believe that he will take over, and it applies not only to ourselves in our spiritual life, but in our pastoral life, in family life, in every kind of life.

And in accepting that Christ takes over, we accept, too, that we do not know—we do not know how to bring the same Christ to the world. I do not know how to convert the world, but I know that he knows, and that he is all-powerful.

The only condition is that I must know I cannot do this. As long as I think, 'Well, I'll do half ... and presently the Lord will come and give a little nudge'—that won't do.

Yet we are always thinking along these lines: 'I'll do my best, and the Lord will come to the rescue.' No, at this depth we have to say: 'I am completely, totally unable.' 'There is no place for human pride in the presence of God.' These are the words of St Paul.

There is indeed no place for human pride in the presence of God.

The first condition, then, is to disappear, to give place to Christ. 'I do not live, Christ lives in me.' Do I accept this? For this is the challenge of the Lord. If I want to be a Christian, let Christ be Christ within me. Let him Christianise through me, evangelise through me, speak through me, act through me. That is the challenge. Once we consent to be a new creature, then the other conditions are easy: they are the logical consequences.

Eyes to see

And if we are to be a new creature, we need new eyes to see, new ears to hear, a new heart to love. This is what I want to say to you tonight. If we wish to be new creatures we need new eyes to see. Faith is nothing other than a new vision—it is seeing with the eyes of the Lord. That is all. It is all, yet it is full of consequence. If we really look, and look at everything imaginable— suffering, contradiction, life, death—with the eyes of Jesus, we completely change our vision.

Yes, we need new eyes to see, if we are new creatures—a new vision to enable us to see, assess, judge, with the eyes of God. It means seeing with the eyes of faith. And faith means penetrating into darkness, seeing things we cannot see with human eyes. Faith is darkness, faith is night, yet in the darkness of faith we can see light and stars.

Suppose there were no night. Suppose that daylight were to go on and on, without our knowing night. If we had not known night we would not have known the stars. Only in the darkness of night are we able to see the stars.

Likewise in the darkness of faith—for faith is a mystery; faith remains full of mysteries—we experience the transcendence of God: we see stars in the darkness. With new eyes, we will see stars more and more.

If you believe

I am only echoing what the Lord has said: 'If you believe, you will see the glory of God.' If you believe, you will see.

That is a paradox. I know, of course, that faith is not seeing. To have faith we must, in some manner, enter into darkness, that is faith. We experience the truth of the Lord's words: 'Blessed are those who have not seen and yet believe.'

On the other hand, the Lord says: 'If you follow me, you will experience my peace and a joy no one will take from you.' We experience the fruits of the Lord's presence—a joy and a peace that no one can take away; yet at the same time we walk in darkness, because faith opens on to the mystery of the Lord.

'If you believe, you will see the glory of God.' This is the key to the three addresses I am to give. We shall try to discover, in the light of faith, the glory of God as the Father, the glory of God as the Son, the glory of God as the Spirit—to see and experience this in darkness and in light at the same time.

Ears to hear

If we need eyes to see, we need ears to hear, just to listen. It is difficult today. We are living in a world of noise, noise, noise! It is difficult to keep silence in the soul, to listen to the voice of the Lord speaking to us.

Think how your room can be filled with music coming from all sorts of places. Yet you do not hear it because you have not turned on the knob of your radio or television. That does not mean the music is not there. It *is* there.

So too, the Lord is present, speaking to you, in large or in small happenings, in all kinds of circumstances, all the time. But we have to listen. What we must ask ourselves, is the Lord saying to us through this or through that? He speaks, usually, through seemingly unimportant occurrences, little coincidences. What, we must ask, is the Lord saying?

I came here by plane. My secretary could not

sit next to me, and that made me feel a bit 'put out!' Then the person sitting beside to me turned out to be the General of a well-known religious order. And so we had a talk. The Lord, it so happened, had something to say to me....

Another time in a plane someone took the place next to me. 'I am Garaudy,' he said. Roger Garaudy is an outstanding Communist intellectual* ... Perhaps you know this. Anyway, we had a wonderful conversation all the way from Brussels to Geneva, about Jesus Christ!

The Lord speaks all the time in ways of this kind. But we have to listen carefully to what he is saying. Remember his words in the Apocalypse: 'Behold, I stand at the door and knock. If anyone hears my voice and opens the door, I will come to him and eat with him, and he with me.'

'If anyone hears my voice.' He speaks slowly, intimately, with respect—provided, that is, we listen (he will not put pressure on us); provided we are willing to respond to his inspiration. But first we have to open our souls, and that means closing our ears to 'atmospherics', 'interferences'. Yes, if we are to hear, we must keep silence, open our souls to prayer—for first and foremost that is what prayer means: silence and openness.

* He was expelled from the P.C.F. (French Communist Party).

To pray, not to inform

To pray is not to 'inform' the Lord. It is not to keep telling the Lord to attend to this and to that problem—to get you through your examinations and so forth! He knows all that! He knows that it matters to you whether on such and such a day your tutor is in a good mood; and all those sort of things.

It is essential you should PRAY to the Lord— not inform him, but put yourself in the right disposition. Only then are you ready to receive the graces he wants to give you; ready to listen when he has something to say to you.

We have to speak to him, yes. But what really matters is that we should listen, that we should make our own the splendid passage in the Old Testament, in the First Book of Kings; describing the encounter between God and the prophet Elijah on the mountain of God, Horeb. The prophet was told:

'Go out and stand on the mountain before Jahweh. And when Jahweh passed by, there came a mighty wind so strong it tore the mountains and shattered the rocks before Jahweh, but Jahweh was not in the wind. After the wind came an earthquake, but Jahweh was not in the earthquake. After the earthquake came a fire, but Jahweh was not in the fire. And after the fire there came the sound of a gentle breeze, and Elijah heard this. He muffled his face in his cloak and went out and stood at the entrance of the cave and a voice came to him.'*

The Lord was not in the earthquake, not in the fire, not in the mighty wind, but he was in the sound of the gentle breeze. We have to know this. We have to open our ears.

A new heart

Finally, we need to be not only new creatures with new eyes to see, new ears to hear. We need a new heart to love. This the Lord himself has explicitly promised to us when he said: 'I will send you my Spirit and I will change your heart of stone' (yes, the Lord is saying: 'Have faith and I'll change that!'. 'I will give you a heart of flesh.'† He is saying: 'I will fill your heart with a living love of myself. My Spirit will give you a heart that is made new.'

We know today what a transplant operation means. Well, something of the kind can be done in the spiritual field. We have to enter into that love with a new heart—the heart of God. Love is a condition—even if we want to see and to hear. Once we love, we see things another will not see.

A mother sees in her children all sorts of

* I Kings XIX vv 11–14.
† Ezekiel XXXVI vv 25–26.

things others do not see, do not notice. Others have not her maternal love. Love opens eyes, helps us to see and to hear. It is a wonderful thing to look at a child speaking to its mother. We don't understand a single word the child is saying, but the mother understands everything! Love is a key to understanding.

Scripture says that love is the key to knowing God. If we do not love God, we will not know him. It is a serious matter if we follow this to its logical conclusion—if we genuinely believe that, unless we love God, we will not understand him, we will not know him. I ponder on this, sometimes, when I find myself in a gathering of learned theologians.

Through prayer we have to become open: this is essential. A true theologian is a man of prayer.

Love is a key

Love is a key that opens the door to faith and hope.

One might suppose that the logical way to spread the Gospel would be first to explain what faith means. Then, after faith, hope. And finally, love and charity. What usually happens, however, is that people discover Jesus through love, through meeting Christians who are loving and to whom, for that reason, they are attracted. Then they ask: 'What is the secret of your love? Why is it that you love in this wonderful way?'

29

May the Christians of today and of tomorrow be able, more and more, to proclaim to the world the secret of their hope and joy and courage: the secret of the Living God within them, as Father, Brother, Breath of life.

May the Lord help me to give to you this testimony during these three days which I shall have the joy of sharing with you!

Lord, we ask you your blessing, that you be very near to each one of these your friends gathered here. Bring them closer to you. Speak yourself, O Lord. You alone know how to speak to them. You know the story of each, their past, their present, their future. You know the goodness that is in them. You know that we are, all of us, Christians, pilgrims on the road. Treat us, O Lord, as you did your disciples on the road to Emmaus. Reveal to us what you revealed to them—that the Scripture was fulfilled in you. They did not know this. Speak, Lord, that we may recognise you, that we may see you, that we may sup with you. Amen.

2

GOD AS MY FATHER

'The Glory of God as my Father'

Lord, we ask first of all that we may listen to you. Nobody can speak about God as Father except you. Nobody knows God, except the Son of God. Nobody knows the Son of God, except the Father. Lord, we enter into the mystery of God as Father. We know all the complexities, all the problems concerning the word 'God'—the meaning of the word and the meaning of God as Father. We ask you humbly to reveal yourself, to manifest yourself: you, our father, to us your children. Amen.

———————

The word father

Dear friends, I feel as if I had known you a very long time, and it gives me joy to begin by reflecting with you on what we mean when we say: 'God is our Father.' We are so used to the word 'father' that perhaps we do not feel, as we should, the freshness contained in it, the note of tenderness with which the word was used by Jesus.

The word 'father'. We think that we know it, yet, in fact, it is always new. Today it is a difficult word to use, just as the word 'God' is difficult. For the last ten years we have heard continually about the death of God. Wherever I went in the

33

United States I heard: 'God is dead.' I met theologians who said: 'God is dead.' Some of those theologians are dead. God is not dead!

That is one point. Then another—a difficulty. What do we mean by 'God'? Many people are searching not only for the meaning of the word 'God'—they are searching for the meaning of the word 'father'. Not only is God dead, so is 'father'.

In our society today we no longer like the word 'father'. We have to thank Freud for that! And so the word 'father' is a bit outmoded: the death of this word is a sympton of our civilisation.

Yet, despite all, we must, I think, with humility and awe, talk about God as 'father'. My Father. Your Father. Our Father.

And I want to try to clarify the meaning of God's paternity: I want to view it first from God's angle—as it were, as God sees it—and then as viewed by ourselves, as a child views it in relation to his father.

Teach us to pray

As you know, one day, when the disciples came to the Lord they put to him this question: 'Lord, John the Baptist teaches his followers to pray. Can you not do the same? Can you not teach *us* to pray?' And you know the answer: 'When you pray, say, "Our Father, who art in heaven, hallowed be thy name, thy kingdom come, thy will be done on earth as it is in heaven" ' And then the Lord continues: 'Give us today our daily bread.'

I think that if we had been left to ourselves to compose the prayer, we would have begun the other way round: 'Our Father who art in heaven, give us today and *as quickly as possible* our daily bread'! And so on. And finally—and I'm not even sure about this—'Hallowed be thy name.'

We have in the words 'Father who art in heaven' a kind of key: an introduction to a dialogue—we ourselves listening, our Father speaking. We want to enter into the relationship that exists between son and father. And this requires in us the disposition to become as children. The kingdom of God will be opened to us only if we react as children—sons and daughters of a father.

That is the way we should be introduced into the mystery of God. We are sons in the Son, we are daughters in Jesus. We approach God as we would a father.

One of your best theologians, C.H. Dodd, explains that the word 'father' implies tenderness, affection, intimacy—as a child might say 'daddy'. It is an invitation to enter into a warm relationship with God.

The maternity of God

The paternity of God. What does this really mean? If we use the word 'father', what, then, about the motherhood of God? Is not this relevant? Is there not something specifically feminine in our concept of God? I would say: 'Yes, in one way there is a feminine element as well as a masculine one.'

When, in addressing God we use the word 'Father', as Jesus told us to, we must not narrow the meaning: we must not put such emphasis on masculinity that we fail to endow God with the tenderness, the affection, the attention characteristic of a mother. When I call God my Father I do so in the knowledge that he loves me with a paternal and a maternal love. Both.

Remember in Holy Scripture how the Lord says: 'If a mother should forget her child, yet I will not forget you.' Yes, God our Father loves us with a maternal love too. You remember, again in Holy Scripture, the conversation between our Lord and his disciples when he said: 'There is no one who has forsaken home, mother, father, brothers, sisters, or land for my sake and for the Gospel who will not receive not only hereafter but even in this world a hundredfold.'

God incorporates into his love for us all the different facets of human love. The love of a father, the love of a mother, the love of a brother, the love of a sister, the love of a husband, the love of a wife—all are present, all are contained in God.

All these human facets are concentrated in God's love for me—in his paternal love: the love of a father, the love of a mother, the tenderness of a sister, the delicacy of a friend. And so, when we say that God is our Father, we believe in him as a loving father, a loving mother, a loving wife, a loving husband, a loving friend.

It is indeed a wonderful thing to know that we encounter in God all the wealth, the variety, the expressions of human love. When I say; 'God is Love,' I mean all that is contained in this immensity.

This being so, I understand the words of St Francis de Sales: 'On the Last Day I would rather be judged by God than by my own mother.'

If I want to reach a deeper understanding of the heart of God, I have to listen to Jesus, who came to reveal to us the heart of his Father. How did Jesus reveal the mystery of the Father? For he is indeed a wonderful teacher. He did not give us learned books: we would have needed an entire library.

I spent this morning in a splendid library in Oxford; yet all the books, wonderful though they are, could not have explained this mystery. Jesus devised another way to teach us the depth psychology of his Father.

The Prodigal Son

He told a story. Perhaps the most moving one in the Gospels: the story of the Prodigal Son.

A parable is invaluable. You are not obliged to understand every word literally, take everything at its face value, analyse the content meticulously. But there is a meaning, a message.

In Rome during the Second Vatican Council I met a well-known Indian theologian. 'What,' I asked him, 'do the people in India think about the Council and our discussions?' I will never forget his answer. 'In India,' he replied, 'they don't think anything about the Council! They don't understand what it is all about!' 'Well then,' I said, 'what ought we to do? How can we make ourselves understood in India?' He answered: 'Couldn't you tell us a parable?'

The Lord told us parables. He told us the most wonderful parable of all: The Prodigal Son. We generally read it in the light of what became of the son—we are interested in him and what he did.

Yet the focus of the parable is not so much on the son as on the father. If you read the story in the light of the father, remembering that the Lord gave us this picture of his own Father, this insight into the heart of the Father is something wonderful.

I would give many books of theology and philosophy for this revelation of the psychology of the Father as given to us in this story by Jesus Christ himself.

The son, we are told, was still a long way off when his father saw him, and the father's heart warmed to his son. The father ran to meet him, flung his arms around him, kissed him and said: 'Let us celebrate, for this son of mine who was dead is restored to life.' Every word of St Luke is music, every word reveals to us the secret of God's paternity.

'He was still a long way off.' God follows each of us when we are still a long way off. The father saw the son in the distance. The son did not see him: he saw the son, for he was standing on high ground. He saw him and his heart went out to him—indeed his heart was already with him. He ran to meet his son. He did not stand waiting. No, he ran and embraced him in a great gesture of love.

Note, he did not give his son time to make a decent act of contrition.—No time for that! He kissed him and said: 'Let us celebrate!'

You will recall the trouble he had with the other son. 'Let us celebrate, for this son of mine was dead and is restored to life.' That did not please the elder son at all.

Let us apply this to ourselves. This is what our heavenly Father is like. When I say: 'Our Father who art in heaven, hallowed be thy name,' I know I will find a father of that kind who sees us from afar off. And when he sees us, you and me and each one of us, his heart will warm to us. He will come running to meet us, take the initiative; fling his arms around the prodigal, kiss him— rejoicing, even if his joy may seem a bit exaggerated! Yes, that is what the elder son felt: he thought his father was being over-emotional, and even unjust.

A different way of judging

And this is an interesting point—to realise that there is no injustice in the Lord: it is simply that he has a different way of judging. A Greek philosopher said long ago that justice comprises treating in an unequal way that which is unequal.

The Lord has his own way of paying his servant, whether he is one who comes at the eleventh hour or at break of day. If there is any question of favouritism, it is to the poor, the failures, the prodigal sons, that the Lord shows favour! And we are all to some degree prodigal sons. It is indeed a wonderful thing and a great joy to know that this is what my Father is like.

A Son of God?

Such, then, is the paternity of God, seen, as it were, from God's angle.

If I reflect upon this same paternity the other

way round, from the human view-point, I must examine myself and really believe that I am the son of the Father: in him, through him, with him—but still a son.

This is my relationship in God. It is difficult to believe that I am a son of God, that he loves me. It is incredible that God—when we think what the word 'God' means—loves each one of us here present, in this gathering; that he loves us personally. It seems strange, impossible.

We feel lost in the immensity of the world. We have only to think of the millions and millions of people here on the earth today: almost four billions! And in the next century? You can work that out for yourselves.

And to think that God is interested in me! I can imagine his giving a morsel of his attention to me, a morsel to you. But that he should give the fullness of his loving attention, in all its entirety, to each one of us, to each one of you—it is beyond belief!

I meet very many people. I have two thousand priests in my diocese. And they expect me to know their names—and their first name! It just isn't possible to know everyone personally, intimately.... I only wish it were! It is, therefore, all the more wonderful to realise that God bestows upon us—upon you and upon me—the totality of his own personal interest.

In the eyes of God, we are not 'one of the crowd'. We are not a drop of water in the ocean. We are not a speck of sand in the desert. In the eyes of God we exist individually.

Loving concern

One of the best definitions I know of charity is that of the French philosopher, Louis Lavelle: *'La charité est une pure attention à l'existence d'autrui.'* 'Charity', he says, 'means giving our undivided attention to the concerns of another.' It is rare to meet persons who can do this.

To give full attention to another is very difficult. Yet God gives this to each one of you. He knows you one by one. He does not get your names mixed up. He knows you by your name, by your first name. He knows the story of your life, chapter by chapter, page by page; he knows every line on every page. He knows even what is written between the lines, and the water-mark on the paper.

You will remember how, in the Gospel, when Jesus meets Nathaniel, he says to him; 'I saw you when you were under the fig tree.' What Nathaniel was doing under the tree we do not know. Perhaps he was in prayer. Anyway, the Lord saw him there! And this is important.

Another example in the Gospel. The Apostles, the week before Easter, say to Jesus: 'Lord, where shall we prepare the Passover

meal?' And he says: 'Go to Jerusalem and you
will meet a man carrying on his shoulder a pit-
cher of water. Follow that man, and where he
goes, you go. It is there I want to celebrate the
Passover.' Just that: Follow. Go where he goes.

Once we are fully convinced that God's loving
concern for us extends to such details, that
means a great deal.

The seventeenth century philosopher Pascal,
in his *Memorial,* puts on the lips of the Lord the
words: *'J'ai verse pour toi telle goutte de mon sang'*—'I
shed for you a drop of my blood'—meaning, a
drop for you, a drop for someone else. In fact,
this is not the real truth at all. God did not shed
a mere drop of his blood for you, another drop
for me. He shed the totality of his blood for each
of us individually, as though each were the only
person in the world.

We must not attribute to God the kind of
mathematical calculations that we go in for.
God's gift to every one of us is complete, total.

In God's eyes we have, each of us, a particular
vocation, unlike that of anyone else. If we do not
play our role ourselves, nobody will replace us.
We are not just anonymous workers in a factory
on a conveyor-belt, where one can take the place
of another, do the same job. Each of us is
required to fulfil a dream of the Lord, respond
to a special call.

Creation itself, the philosopher Leon Brunschvicg says, is an idea of the Lord, an expression of the Lord. *'Le monde est une pensée qui ne se pense pas, suspendue à une pensée qui se pense.'* In the sight of God, then, 'the world is a thought, unthought, depending upon a thought which is thought.'

It is of the utmost importance we should be aware that God seeks out you and me, in the most unexpected ways. He was disguised as a gardener when he met Mary Magdalen on Easter morning. She mistook him for a gardener. He met the two disciples on the road to Emmaus, just as if he were an ordinary traveller.

A love story

God creates for each one of us a love story. You know Eric Segal's novel *Love Story?* Well, there is a love story in the mind of God for each of us.

Yes, life is a novel. God invents the most unexpected things. I never expected to be here. And I imagine that for you it was a bit unexpected too. All the time God is inventing, creating and writing a novel with the lives of each one of you....

I don't know if you are tempted, when reading a book—particularly if it is a thriller—to turn to the last page to find out who was the murderer! It's not fair on the author. You should turn the pages one at a time, not look at the end. When you have finished the book, you will notice, if you read it again, a whole series of happenings which escaped your attention and would have pointed out to you who the murderer was.

In a way, that is how it is with us. The Lord will make the meaning of our lives clear to us only in the final chapter, when the last line has been written.

Gabriel Marcel, the French philosopher, said: *'La vie est une phrase dont on ne comprend le sens que lorsque le dernier mot est dit.'* 'Life may be compared to a sentence the meaning of which is clear only when the last word has been spoken.'

It will indeed be a great surprise to discover the wonderful love of the Lord for you and for me.

The mystery of suffering

There still remains the problem of suffering.

Yes, we are still confronted by a mystery: the mystery of God's love and human liberty. The only words that, for me, shed light upon the darkness are those of the poet Paul Claudel. 'Jesus,' he says, 'did not come to explain away suffering or to remove it. He came to take it upon himself, to assume human suffering and fill it with his presence.' All I can say is: the existence of God's love is so real that I cannot doubt even in the midst of darkness.

When I see a ray of the sun, I know the sun is there. I cannot explain the darkness of the sky, but one ray of light is enough to tell me the sun is behind the clouds.

Looking at our life with the eyes of faith, we will experience the truth of the words of St Paul: 'For those whom God loves, all things work together for good.' Not only for good, but for the best.

The best answer

This means, also, that God's answer to our prayers is always the best answer. But it does not mean that God will grant what I ask. He can do precisely the opposite. Yet I know that God will hear my prayer, because he loves me more than I love myself. God's answer, I am certain, will be the best he can give. From time to time we experience this in an unforgettable way.

Take the life of St Augustine. One night his mother, Monica, was praying in a chapel on the coast of Africa—she spent the whole night in prayer in that little chapel by the sea—begging the Lord that her son, who was very young at the time, would not leave Africa and go to Rome, the city of perdition. She prayed and prayed, and at that very moment, while she was praying in the chapel, Augustine seized the opportunity to board a ship and sail for Rome.

Now, if anyone were to say that she prayed in vain, that her prayer went unanswered, that would be quite wrong. Augustine had to go to

Rome—not to stay there, but to go on to Milan, to meet St Ambrose, find the faith, and become the great saint that he later was. In fact, God moved heaven and earth to answer Monica's prayer, but not in the way she imagined—quite the contrary!

I don't know what each of you will do in heaven, but one of the things I shall certainly do is thank the Lord for the many times he did *not* answer my prayers in the way I hoped for. We must believe that the providence of God, in his wisdom, accompanies us from the very beginning of life until the end.

Disposing all things

In the liturgy in the week before Christmas, we have the wonderful antiphon in which we say: *'O Sapientia... attingens a fine usque ad finem, fortiter suaviterque disponens omnia.'* 'O Wisdom, arranging and disposing all things, from the beginning to the very end, powerfully, yet gently.'

Yes, God in his wisdom is powerful, yet gentle, attendant upon us always, everywhere, from within, not from without. God does not interfere with human liberty. It is not a matter of God doing his part, I doing mine. No: what I do, I do totally myself, but God is there too, in his totality, in a manner all his own. He acts at a level so deep that he does not meddle in our liberty, and yet he is present, directing the circumstances of our lives.

Once we open our eyes in a spirit of faith, we can recognise God's presence. Signs can be sudden. They can also be slow, gradual, and discreet. Sometimes all becomes clear only after a while. But once our eyes are open, once our ears catch the whisper of the breeze, once the heart is touched with understanding (to love is to understand), then we see the Lord where others will say: 'it's just chance!' No, the Lord is there, *incognito!*

Suppose I were to take, say, a fistful of pins and throw them up into the air. It is possible that every pin, when it falls to the ground, will stand upright. It is possible—mathematically. But I can be sure it will not happen.

For every occurrence we can find an explanation. Why did I meet that particular person at that particular time? I can give an explanation that is perfectly valid. Yet, behind it, I can see the Lord at work. Sometimes I do not see this at once, only later. Sometimes one little sign can be enough.

Signs

I imagine—you must know this better than I do!—that if a young man and a girl fall in love, there is no need for many signs to show what is happening. One small sign suffices.

When I was Vice-Rector at the University of

Louvain I would notice a student saying to a girl sitting next to him: 'Would you lend me your note-book?' Or: 'I'd like to borrow your notes.' Well, if it happened once, you attached no importance to it. But when it happened several times... well, everyone knew what to think! A little sign. Love has opened the eyes.

Similarly, if I find a match in the desert, I know that a traveller has been there. Just one match: that is enough. And if I see a footprint in the snow, a single footprint—well, that is a sign. Again, if I see one ray of sunlight, I know, even if the sky is overcast, that the sun is there, as I have said, behind the clouds.

Likewise, we recognise the signs of God in our own lives.

Sometimes, also, death comes in a strangely appropriate manner (it would take too long to tell you how often I have noticed this), as if God, in his graciousness, had, in the moment of death, set his seal upon a life particularly dear to him.

And why not, if God loves us from the beginning to the end? It is not at all surprising. I cannot, of course, prove this. But at times I have said to myself: 'That was a kind gesture of the Lord!'

Take Teilhard de Chardin. As everyone knows, he laid tremendous stress on the meaning of Easter. His books are steeped in faith in the cosmic Christ, and in the Resurrection. Easter, one could say, was the life of his life. Well, as you

know, he died in New York, almost unknown—
on Easter Sunday! I can't but feel that, here, was
the hand of the Lord.

Or think of Dom Odo Casel O.S.B., who for
twenty five years strove to restore the mystery to
the liturgy of Easter Saturday, thus anticipating
the Pascal understanding of the Eucharist as
stressed in the Second Vatican Council.

When he died in 1948 in a Benedictine chapel
during the Easter Vigil, at that very moment the
choir began to sing the glorious Paschal hymn:

Exultet iam angelica turba caelorum.

I like to think that this did not go unnoticed in
heaven. . . if it were a mere smile.

You are free to interpret such things as you
will. But once in your own experience you have
come across something of this sort, you feel
bound to say: 'The Lord was there.'

The tapestry of life

I still remember from my boyhood a sermon
by a Capuchin friar—a bad sermon, I think—
who spoke with great vehemence about eternity.

From the recurrent thought of eternity, fired
by that very ordinary sermon, my vocation to the
priesthood was, I think, born.

As to the working of providence in my later
life, it would be difficult and would take too long

to tell you the whole story. So let me tell you just this. When I do not know what to say to the Lord in prayer, I compose a litany made up of the many, many things for which I have to be thankful to him.

Sometimes I think of life (and you can do the same) as resembling a tapestry. If you look at the reverse side, while the weavers are at work, the many different threads give an impression of chaos. To understand, you have to wait until the tapestry is finished. Then when you turn it around and look at the other side, you see the picture! You realise that every thread contributed to this, that every one had a meaning, a purpose.

I could take one of the threads in my own life: the ecumenical thread. How did the Lord prepare me to work in this sphere? To answer, I must look back to a predecessor of mine: Cardinal Mercier. It was he who chaired the Malines Conversations: the first dialogue between the Anglican Communion and the Church of Rome. Informal discussions, but rich in meaning and possibilities. Think of the courage of the two leading men: Lord Halifax on the Anglican side, Cardinal Mercier on the Catholic. Think how they met in what is now my residence in Malines, thus breaking a silence that had lasted four centuries. Think, too, of the misunderstanding, the sufferings, arising out of that silence!

It would be tedious for you were I to attempt to speak in detail of my part in ecumenism. It suffices to say that I have been aware in my life of what I can only call a 'sense of ecumenical continuity'—God's providence, in that sphere, leading me from one stage to the next. God, I firmly believe has been 'behind the scenes.'

Now for each of you here tonight it is the same. God is always at hand, loving you, caring for you. His providence, whether visible or invisible, does not fail.

Such is my message.

Help us, O Lord, to believe that you are very near to us, that you are our Father, our loving Father, that you care for each one of us every day of our lives, that nothing escapes your attention—the fullness of your attention, the fullness of your love. We thank you, Lord, for loving us so much. Our only difficulty is, Lord, that it is so wonderful. But we believe that God is wonderful. We thank you, Lord, because you are wonderful in our lives and in yourself. Amen.

3

THE LIVING SON, MY BROTHER'

'The Glory of God as the Living Son,
my Brother'

No one can speak about you, Lord, except in and with the Holy Spirit. You alone, Holy Spirit, can pronounce the name of Jesus. No one can say Jesus is Lord except in the Holy Spirit. Holy Spirit, you were sent to lead us in the fullness of the mystery of our Lord, our Saviour, our Redeemer. Holy Spirit, you came to make alive Jesus Christ. Help us today to glorify the Son. Amen.

God as my Brother

I want to speak this evening about the Son of God as my Brother. I want to begin with a passage of Holy Scripture.

Jesus is walking with his Apostles in the country around Caesarea, when he suddenly puts to them the crucial question: 'Who do men say the Son of Man is?'

You know the answer: 'Some say that you are John the Baptist. Others say you are Elias. Others say you are Jeremiah or one of the prophets.'

Then comes the question, the straight question of the Lord to his disciples: 'And who do *you* say I am?' Simon Peter answers in the name of them all: 'You are the Messiah, the Son of the living God.'

Ever since that moment, this same question has been put by the Lord in a mysterious way to each generation. And the same question, 'Who do you say I am—I, the Lord Jesus Christ?' has been answered in a variety of ways.

Abstractions

We must resist the temptation to talk about Christianity as if we were speaking about an '–ism,' as we speak of Marxism or Hegelism. We have become accustomed to these abstractions.

Christianity is not an '–ism.' It is not first and foremost a set of doctrines. First and foremost it involves a person: 'Who do you say I am?'

In Jesus, the messenger and the message are one. Jesus is the message in his own person. And it is not only what he says which is important, but everything he does or refuses to do.

Yes, everything is important. The way he was born. What he did on the road to Jerusalem. How he suffered. How he died. All this is part of the message. All this is contained in the unity of his person—the person who is himself the Message Incarnate.

We are tempted by abstractions. I remember, soon after the Second Vatican Council, putting to the distinguished German theologian, Karl Rahner, the question: 'How do you explain a sort of aloofness on the part even of many Roman Catholics, when one touches upon the subject of Mary?' His answer was, I thought striking, and it remains relevant here. 'One of the reasons,' he said, 'is that so many of us are turning Christianity more and more into an abstraction.' Then he added: 'And abstractions do not need a mother!'

In the midst of you there is someone whom you do not know

Jesus is not an abstraction. Christianity is not an abstraction. 'Who do you say I am?' What John the Baptist said in his day is still true in our times: 'In the midst of you there is someone whom you do not know.'

Jesus has been present in every generation for twenty centuries. He is always 'here,' living,— more real than we are ourselves. His mysterious presence is with us. 'In the midst of you there is someone whom you do not know.'

We must try to approach the Lord as a *person,* in a spirit of faith, in all reverence, knowing that human words are faltering; knowing that Jesus is and remains for ever the mystery of God—Love become Man.

I want first of all to stress the relevance today of this same question: 'Who do you say I am?' At first sight, it may not seem to be a question for today. It does not seem to concern us. The questions put in our world are not about God. Even if people talk about God, they speak about his name, ask about the possibility of knowing him. Even so, the question of God is not, for the majority of people, it must be admitted, in the forefront of today's problems.

The great concern at the present time is not: 'Who is Jesus Christ?' Attention is focussed elsewhere. People do not ask, 'What about God?' but 'What about man?'

What about man?

That is our problem, now. What about man? What is the meaning of man? From first to last, questions range from the unborn child to the moment of death. The right to be born and the right to die—this is what attracts attention in the daily papers. What is the meaning of man? What is the meaning of mankind, of humanity? What is the future of our society? What will the year 2000 be like?

I am always impressed when I see young people preoccupied with the future of the world. It is, of course, a problem which immediately concerns us all.

Yet why should we talk about Jesus Christ, a man of the past, a man of twenty centuries ago? Why should we make the effort to answer the question posed by him, even if we find the subject an intriguing one?

We should, I think, make it clear that our purpose in talking about Jesus Christ rests on the fact that in doing so we are talking about man: to discover Jesus is to discover man. It is, therefore, all the more important to know what kind of man Jesus Christ is.

In him alone we shall understand ourselves.

Fundamental questions

He gives the final answer to the ultimate, human, global question. He does not come—he has not come—to answer our technical or scientific problems. No, we must avoid reading into the Scriptures what is not there. He has come to give a clear answer to fundamental questions.

What, for instance, is the meaning of mankind? In other words, what is man? Why do I exist? What is the meaning of suffering? What is the meaning of death? What awaits us after death? These are fundamental questions, relevant for all times, for all seasons.

I like the title of a book by the German philosopher, Max Scheler: *Von Ewigen im Menschen*. It could be translated: *The Eternal Man*.

Generation follows generation, questions vary according to circumstances. Yet behind changing humanity is an unchanging man asking always the same questions. What am I doing here? What meaning is there in all this? Is there any reason to take life seriously? What, in the last analysis, is the explanation of the problems, the questions, entailed? Camus said once: 'There is only one question, namely, why not to commit suicide?'

A reason to live?

The late Robert Kennedy said that the problem facing youth in the United States is that they have everything except a reason to live.

We look at Jesus because in him we find a reason to live, to suffer, to die. That, for me, is Jesus. In the Gospel, Jesus says that he is the Truth, the Way, the Life.

Yes, Lord, you are the living truth. My life makes no sense without you. You are the living way—you not only show me the way, you accompany me along the way. You are in me, with me, as I walk. You are the reason for my existence, the reason for my hope, the reason for my joy!

Without Jesus Christ we do not know ourselves. If the world's attention is focussed on man, it must also be focussed on Jesus, the Son of Man, the Son of the living God. We need him if we are to understand ourselves.

Pascal in *Les Pensées* says that we don't know God except *through* Jesus Christ, and that we don't know ourselves except *in* Jesus Christ. Only through him do we know the meaning of life and of death. Without Jesus Christ we know neither God nor ourselves.

During the last decade we heard much learned

talk about the 'death of God.' We are now confronted with the problem of the death of man
or, in other words, the survival of man. That is
why we should look at Jesus Christ, because in
him we find the hope of a new humanity.

'Who do you say I am?' Yes, I believe that for
our time this question is more relevant than
ever.

The answer of Peter

And now—the answer to that question? It is
still the answer of Peter as we find it in the
Gospel. Illumined by the light of Easter and by
the light of Pentecost, we Christians of today can
only repeat: 'You are the Son of the living God.'

The same answer was expressed, in terms of
dogma, as you know, at the Council of Nicaea in
the fourth century, in a clear statement about
the divinity of Christ. Then, in the fifth century,
at the Council of Chalcedon, came a clear
statement about Christ's human nature.

That same answer, given at Nicaea and
Chalcedon, remains in essence for ever. We
know that formulations can change, but the
message contained in them cannot change.

Look at the faith of your Church

Twenty centuries have passed, and the answer
of Peter remains unchanged. This means a lot. I
am always moved during the celebration of the

Eucharist when, just before the reception of Holy Communion, I say to the Lord in the words of the liturgy: 'Lord, do not look at my faith, do not look at my sins, but look at the faith of your Church.'

This gives to my own individual and inadequate faith another perspective, another dimension. 'Lord, I come to you, not with this inadequate, personal faith, but with the faith of twenty centuries, with the faith of Mary and the Apostles, with the faith of Peter and Paul, the martyrs, the confessors, and the doctors of the Church—the faith down the centuries of the saints and all who were united in your name.' This is something tremendous, something inspiring.

I wish to go a step further. This, after twenty centuries of faith, is the answer. But we are entitled to ask another question: 'What exactly is the meaning of this answer?' At one and the same time, Jesus is divine and human. We speak of Jesus as the unique Son of the living God. We also speak of Jesus as being truly human—as our Brother.

I want, tonight, to try, not to answer, not to explain—we cannot do that—but to attempt, in fear and trembling, to approach the mystery of the divine nature of Christ. Here, more than ever, we should obey the words spoken by the angel to Moses: 'Put off your shoes, for the ground on which you tread is holy.'

Yes, the ground on which we tread is holy. We have to be aware that we are approaching a burn-
ing bush. We are approaching in Christ the con-
crete manifestation, in time and space, of the transcendence of God.

A *living parable*

I am making a strong affirmation, I realise, in saying that the words, actions, attitudes—indeed all that transpires in the life of Jesus—are the translation into concrete reality of the purpose of a gracious Father in relation to his creation.

All that we have said about the love of God as a Father—all this we find in Jesus Christ, ex-
pressed, translated into human terms, so that it is possible for us to understand the living parable which is none other than Jesus himself.

The Word became flesh. And so all that per-
tains to him—to Jesus as man, is at the same time a proclamation of God.

The loving concern of Jesus for the woman taken in adultery, the forgiveness manifested on the Cross, the parable of the Prodigal Son, the warmth of his relationship with Martha, Mary, and Lazarus, John and the others: all this is more than just an exemplary human approach to life.

Certainly it tells us about the life of man and how that life should be led, but more important, it tells us about the attitude of God towards man and towards life. In Jesus we see the image of God, the living, concrete, and transcendent manifestation of God, revealed in human terms.

Jesus is, essentially, the Son of the Father. He is the expression of the Father. He is the splendour, and the glory of the Father.

'The concerns of my Father'

Remember what Jesus said to the Apostle Philip: 'Who sees me sees the Father.' The life of Jesus was completely orientated towards the Father. Remember his words, while he was still a boy when he was lost, then found, in the Temple: 'I have to be about the concerns of my Father.'

And in the Scriptures we read that Jesus came to tell us about his Father. When he leaves the Apostles to face his passion and crucifixion, he says before going: 'Now let us go, so that the world may see I love my Father.'

He does not say: 'that the world may see I love mankind.' At that moment, his passion is indeed a tremendous act of love for mankind, but in the depth of his soul there is, as it were, a priority: the glory of his Father: 'I am ready to die, to accept suffering,' he is saying, 'that the world may know I love the Father.'

This relationship of Son to Father crowns all he does—is, indeed, its supreme expression. It is

64

the fullness of his humanity.

The divine nature of Christ

Why, people ask, is it so important to stress the divine, as well as the human, nature of Christ? Is it not enough to accept that he was a great and remarkable prophet—to accept, even, that he came to save us? You remember the Jesus Movement—the Jesus Freaks? Those who belonged to this movement acknowledged Jesus as a prophet. They even acknowledged him as having saved them from drugs and all sorts of evils in society.

But the question arises: 'Have we to go a step further? Is there a reason why we should be interested in the divinity of one who, we concede, is a prophet and a saviour?'

To answer this, we have to understand, I think, that if Jesus is not, as we say in the Creed he is, 'true God from true God', we do not, in that case, know God in human terms. If Jesus were human only, then he could only tell us, as it were second-hand, about God: a God who is as remote from us as the immutable 'mover' of Aristotle. For if Jesus were not divine, he could speak about God only from outside. It is important we should know, in human terms, something of the intimacy, the inner nature, of God himself.

I remember the words of Bossuet—striking

words: *'Il est né dans ce secret et dans cette gloire.'*
'Jesus was born,' he says, 'in the secrecy of his
Father's glorious intimacy.' Born there, enjoying
so intimate a relationship with his Father, that
he tells us, when he speaks, something first-
hand, not second-hand. If Jesus were only a
man, if God sent us a Saviour from outside only,
without involving himself in a personal manner,
then he would remain detached—at a distance
from us.

Suffering in the sight of God?

To appreciate what I mean, you should look, I
think, at the picture chosen for your Mission,
showing Jesus on his way to be crucified. There
you see something of what suffering means in
the sight of God.

I cannot explain suffering. One thing I can
say: God took it upon himself to follow this way
—one that is not foreign to us, not outside our
experience. He chose this. He became the man
of suffering, so that he could enter THAT WAY
into the mystery of death and resurrection. He is
on our side. And if God is on our side, that
changes the perspective.

God has not sent a messenger or representative to help the poor creatures we are—he has
involved himself. It is in his nature to redeem his
own creation.

That is what God is like.

Unless we understand that Jesus is truly human, we cannot understand the depth of God's love. And unless we understand that Jesus is truly divine, we cannot understand the depth of God's love.

Our God is near us. Our God is far removed from the God of deism. Ours is the God of Jesus Christ, the God and Father of Jesus Christ.

An American writer has said that moral philosophy is not religion. Nor, he goes on, is social 'do-gooding.' Nor is working for peace or racial integration. To follow Christ as one might follow Socrates or Gandhi (men whose lives and precepts deserve to be imitated and followed)— not even this is religion.

Nothing indeed can claim to be religion, as distinct from philosophy, worthy conduct and the like, unless it can be said to derive from God's revelation of himself and from the operation of his grace in our lives. And religion conceived of in this way cannot be secularised.

The humanity of Christ

And now I want to look with you at the humanity of the Lord.

The mystery of the Incarnation means that we believe, not only in the divinity of Christ but also in his full humanity. We are required to accept both—not permitting the exaggeration of one at the expense of the other. The two are distinct, but indissoluble.

Yet there will always be something in the nature of a tension. We see this down the centuries, according as to whether greater stress is laid on Christ's human or on his divine nature. We will always have the school of Antioch or the school of Alexandria,* depending upon where the emphasis is laid at a given moment.

There will always be a tension between the *homo assumptus* and the *verbum caro*—some stressing that God has become man, others that man has become divinised. We have to maintain the balance firmly, and resist the temptation to go from one extreme to the other.

As you know, when something is repeated over and over again for a long time, there is, automatically, a risk of falsification, of exaggeration. Then the day comes when there is a reaction—a swing of the pendulum. In the recent past there was a reaction against a tendency to diminish the humanity of Christ. Stress, therefore, was put, and rightly so, on his human nature. Next came an excessive reaction in the opposite direction. That is what happens.

We have to shun the temptation to stress

* Theologians of the School of Antioch (4th and 5th centuries) stressed, within the limitations of orthodoxy, the human dimension of Christ. In contrast theologians of the School of Alexandria stressed the divine dimension of Christ; man's predicament is viewed essentially rather than existentially.

Christ's divinity at the expense of his humanity. Or the other way round. We have to be clear that Jesus is not, as we are inclined to think, perhaps unconsciously, 'fifty-fifty'—fifty human and fifty divine.

Totally divine, totally human

No. That is not the mystery of the Incarnation. We believe Jesus to be born totally divine and totally human. We do not mean that, in Jesus, God is endowed with an appearance of humanity—this would be a *theophania*: God appearing in a kind of human garment. That, I repeat, is not the mystery of the Incarnation.

It is important to realise that Jesus is human, not in spite of his divinity, but because of his divinity. Here is to be found the key to our understanding of the nature of Jesus Christ.

Let us pause to meditate upon the Lord in his divinity and in his humanity—so that you may have time to concentrate, in prayer and silence, upon the answer to the question: 'Who do you say I am, my friends?' 'Who do you say I am?'— to each one of you.

When I look at the humanity of Jesus Christ, I see in him the heart of the human creation. You remember what St Paul said in his Epistle to the Colossians:

'He is the image of the invisible God. In him everything in heaven and earth was created. All things, all together in him, in him the complete being of God by God's own choice came to dwell.'

Remember the words: 'God was in Christ, reconciling to himself the world.' That is Jesus Christ: the centre of creation; the summit of humanity.

Human nature, it has been said, is the *grammatica*—the 'spelling out' or pronouncement of God's word in time. Our destiny is expressed in him: the mystery of creation and the Incarnation.

God said: 'Let us make man in our image, after our likeness.' The man Jesus Christ is that image, that unique likeness. He revealed in his own unique way the mystery and purpose of the creation of humanity—namely, that man be capable of seeing God: *homo capax Dei.*

And as to the Incarnation, it is of inestimable value to meditate on the words of Psalm 8:

'What is man that you are mindful of him?
The son of man that you should care for him?
Yet you have made him little less than God
And you have crowned him with glory and honour.'

We see Jesus in this psalm.

We have to understand that we are men in that man, that we are sons in this Son; that we are 'little less than God'; that in Jesus Christ the 'little less' is nullified.

Jesus in the Saints

Before leaving you, I would like to reflect a moment more upon the humanity of the Lord. To appreciate the humanity of Jesus we have only to turn over, one after another, the pages of the Gospel. There we see how human Jesus is. With this aspect we are all familiar. I would like, however, to think also of an aspect of his humanity that is revealed to us in another sphere—in the lives, that is, of the saints.

Both in the past and today, Christianity means: 'I do not live, Christ lives in me.' I should find, therefore, in those who are true Christians a special touch of humanity. The wonderful humanity of the Lord is, surely to be expected.

Take any saint you like. The saints are a living gospel. They cry the Gospel with their lives. They are a facet of Christ's humanity. They are a unique experience of God in man.

A pilgrim coming back from Ars, a small town in France, near Lyon, put into very simple words what he felt after meeting there the saintly parish priest who, as you know, cared deeply for pilgrims, gave a warm welcome to every sinner.

71

This pilgrim exclaimed: *'J'ai vu Dieu dans un homme.'* 'I saw God in a human being.' In the soul of the Curé of Ars Jesus was alive.

God is indeed wonderful in his saints. They are not wonderful in themselves: God is wonderful in them.

I would like to share with you, in this sphere, a few experiences of my own. For I have had during my life the grace of meeting from time to time persons whom I sincerely believe to be saints. It is risky, I know, to use the word 'saint' of those who are still living—and they would certainly be upset if I were to give their names. And so I will at least try not to give names... It is easier to talk of persons who are dead.

As to the living, I could, I think, nevertheless apply the word 'saint' to, say, ten persons in different parts of the world—Europe, Latin America, Asia, Canada, the United States. I mention countries to indicate that a common denominator, as it were, unites these persons, widely separated as they are.

When I meditate on what they have in common, I can only say: 'Christ lives in them.' I am conscious of a kind of 'depossession' of self—humility, if you like.

Humility is endless'
In a sense, the saints seem not to exist for themselves. This has always struck me. They have

no wish to be in the limelight. They are what they are—non-existing, just letting the Lord act in and through them with a love which has a quality all its own: a particular motivation. They do not love only for the sake of God, but with the heart of God.

Their love for others is firm, steadfast, rock-like, immovable. It asks nothing in return. It does not expect a 'Thank you.' It is fidelity under another name. It is a love that is indifferent to reactions. Always waiting. Always hoping. Always confident that, ultimately, things will be well.

The saints—I notice this too—combine a universal love with a deeply personal love. They love everyone, and yet they love individually. They are attentive to you personally. They are more interested in you than you are in yourself!

The humour of the saints

Those whom I have in mind—all of them—have a sense of humour. Is that important? you may ask. It is, because it makes them human. Perhaps you know a book called *L'Humour chez les Saints. Humour of the Saints.*

There is a long tradition of humour among the saints. Think only of Thomas More! Or Philip Neri! And Pope John XXIII, of whom I was privileged to see a good deal—I said I'd try not to give names, but there it is! You'd think he didn't exist! He never obtruded himself. He would speak about 'the Pope', just as anyone else would. He was the absolute reverse of the *grand seigneur*. He was perfectly natural.

Pope John is a dangerous topic. I could tell stories about him for hours on end. Here's just one, to show you how human he was. Bishop Fulton Sheen had an audience with the Pope for eleven in the morning. He was received at twelve. Meanwhile, as he sat waiting in a parlour, he was aware of a lot of noise on the other side of a door and many comings and goings. The first official photographs of the Pope, it transpired, were being taken. Apologising, later, for the delay, Pope John said: 'I don't understand the Lord. I don't understand God at all. He knew from all eternity that I would be Pope. Why, then, didn't he make me more photogenic!'

Mother Teresa and Dom Helder Camara

In August this year at a Eucharist World Congress at Philadelphia, two persons were the centre of attraction: Mother Teresa of Calcutta and Dom Helder Camara. It was felt there was something special about them, something specially human. When they both appeared on television, the interviewer began attacking Mother Teresa. 'We don't mind *you*, Mother Teresa. You love the poor.... But what about the wealth of the Vatican?—and the Church?' and so on.

It was a violent attack. And Mother Teresa's reaction was typical. She just looked at the speaker, and said: 'Sir, you can't be happy: you're so angry. Something is upsetting you. You're not at peace.'

'And what,' he asked, 'can I do to change that?'

'Well,' she replied, 'you should have faith. Faith will help you.'

'And how do I get faith? What do I have to do?'

And on television, standing there, she said, 'You should pray.'

'I can't pray,' he told her.

'Well, then we'll pray for you!' she replied.

Helder Camara wanted to express to Mother Teresa the admiration of the Church for what she is doing for the poor in India. And so he went on to the platform to kiss her hands. Mother Teresa demurred, and Dom Helder spoke to her. He told me afterwards what he had said... 'Mother Teresa, have you never read the story of Peter and Jesus—when Jesus wanted to wash Peter's feet?' 'Oh, yes,' she said—she understood that.

In one instance after another you see the same kind of thing. The humanity of Christ living down the centuries.

The love of Christ shines in a special way in Mother Teresa of Calcutta. I mention her by name—one on my private list—only to give you an example of love and humour in a true disciple of Jesus Christ.

Again during the Eucharistic Congress in Philadelphia, she told the following story, which needs no comment:

'Some professors came to our house in Calcutta. "Tell us something," one of them said, "that would change our lives." And I said, "Smile at each other." then one of them asked me—(a strange question): "Are you married?"* "Yes." I said. "And I sometimes find it very difficult to smile at Jesus. He can be so demanding!"

'And I repeated: "Smile at each other. Smile at people you live with—it's easy to smile at strangers." '

A smile is a human touch.

To smile is something we can all do. And so, we have, here, an invitation to translate into daily life the wonderful humanity of our Lord.

In one instance after another, in the Saints, you see the same kind of thing.

Lord, we thank you because you are so human, because you are so close to us, because you bring us into the heart of your Father. Bless, O Lord, all of us who are here. Make us one in your love for the Father and for all mankind. Amen.

* According to an ancient tradition a nun is said to be a 'bride of Christ'. The same is said of the Church.

4

THE HOLY SPIRIT, MY BREATH OF LIFE

*'The Glory of God as The Holy Spirit,
my Breath of Life'*

We should listen, first of all, to the Lord as he announces the coming of the Holy Spirit.

At the end of the Last Supper he says to his disciples:

'I have still much I could say to you, but the burden would be too heavy for you now. When, however the Spirit of Truth comes, he will guide you into all truth, for he will not speak on his own authority: he will tell you only what he hears, and make known to you the things that are to come. He will glorify me, for everything he makes known to you he will draw from what is mine. All that the Father has is mine and that is why I said, everything he makes known to you he will draw from what is mine.'

Lord, you promised you would send your Spirit. Pentecost is the answer to your promise. Lord, we ask you to help us to enter into the mystery of the Holy Spirit, the mystery of Pentecost: the Pentecost of the past, the Pentecost of today, the Pentecost of the future. Amen.

The breath of my life

I shall talk tonight about God as the Breath of my life. This means I shall talk to you about the Holy Spirit, who is the Breath of life of the Father and the Son, who is the Love of the Father for the Son and the Love of the Son for the Father. We are loved by the Father in the Son and in the Holy Spirit.

We know the Holy Spirit. And yet we have to confess that we do not know him. It is easier to speak about God as our Father. It is easier to be clear about him because we know what the word 'father' means. It is easier, also, to understand what is meant by the Son of God and by brotherhood with Jesus.

The meaning of the Holy Spirit is more mysterious. We have to discover afresh the meaning and the role of the Holy Spirit for us today.

Sometimes we are tempted to say that the Holy Spirit comes to take the place of Jesus. When Jesus went away, he announced the coming of the Spirit. And so there is a tendency to think that the Spirit came to fill the absence of the Lord. No, he did not come to fill the absence of Jesus Christ. He came to perfect his presence, which is quite different.

He came to bring Jesus out of the past and make him present today. The glorification of Jesus included the sending of the Spirit. And, through the Spirit, what Jesus did within the limitations of time and space in his own country, has become a universal mission. Through the Holy Spirit, Jesus, spanning time and space, is with us at this very moment.

On the death of some well-known person we are impressed when we hear on the radio a speech made by the man who has died. It is strange to listen to the voice of someone no longer on earth. A voice coming out of the past is impressive.

Now, the Holy Spirit brings alive all the words we read in the Gospel, all that Jesus said twenty centuries ago. He brings all this to life, proclaiming to us a message for today. This is not romanticising. It is faith.

It is the role of the Holy Spirit to make Jesus Christ present in every generation, here and now: to give him actuality, make him contemporaneous. This is what the Spirit accomplishes, bringing the past into the full light of the present, at the same time preparing for the future.

Past, present, and future. We experience this in a special way in the Eucharist. Through the working of the Holy Spirit, the Eucharist is a memorial of the past, a present actuality, an anticipation of the future, preparing us for the coming of the Lord in his full glory. That is the work of the Spirit in time and on into eternity.

Come, Holy Spirit

And now I would like to consider what the
Spirit comes to do today, and what should be the
meaning of our liturgical prayer when we say:
'Come, Holy Spirit, and you will renew the face
of the earth!'

To renew the face of the earth we have to
begin at the beginning. And the beginning is
ourselves. We are tempted to forget that the first
step towards renewing the face of the world is to
renew ourselves: to renew, in the world today,
our faith as Christians. I have never met anyone
who reproaches us for being Christians: we are
reproached for not being Christian enough!

That is our problem. To be renewed. It is a
long story: the story of twenty centuries. We
carry our treasure in frail vessels: twenty centuries of history show that Christians have not
always shouldered their responsibilities. We have
to go back to the beginning. We have to return
to the beginning of Christianity—to the morning
of Pentecost. We have to return to when the
Holy Spirit came down.

There is a book called *Nine o'clock in the Morning,*
by Dennis Bennett.

We know that Pentecost took place at precisely
nine o'clock, for when Peter and the Eleven
came down from the Upper Room, people said:
'They're drunk!' 'No,' answered Peter, 'no one is
drunk at nine o'clock in the morning!' And so,

thanks to the Lord, we know the exact hour of Pentecost: nine o'clock in the morning.

That is where we have to start.

'What are we to do?'

When Peter had ended the first 'sermon' in the history of the Church, the crowd, you will remember, said to him and to the Eleven gathered around him: 'Friends, what are we to do?' That indeed is the question. And it is valid today for each of us.

'Repent!' Peter said. 'Be baptised in the name of Jesus and you will receive the gift of the Holy Spirit.'

Repent! This is an invitation to conversion. All of us have to be converted. And converted again and again. You know the saying of St Francis de Sales: 'Pride—human pride—dies a quarter of an hour after our own death!' And so the invitation is always there: 'Repent! Repent of your weaknesses. Repent of what we are!'

And we have to admit, all of us, that we are sinners. I have in my library a book called: *Whatever became of Sin?* by Karl Manninger. What indeed?

Nobody talks about sin any more. There are all sorts of explanations for this. Yet we have to admit that we are sinners. We do so at the beginning of the liturgy, in a ritualistic form. We who are Roman Catholics used to do so in Latin. It is much more comfortable to say a *Confiteor*—to use a Latin word! But truly to repent requires us to be aware that we are sinners.

To help you to this awareness may I quote G.K. Chesterton's definition of a saint? 'A saint,' he says, 'is someone who knows that he is a sinner.' That perhaps can be an encouragement to us to acknowledge, to confess, what we are—sinners. Repent!

The opportunity offered to you

Take the opportunity offered to each one of you by the Mission. I ask you this in the name of the Lord.

In the light of the Lord, ponder on your life—its weaknesses, but also on what you are prepared to give. You have to pay a price if you want to enter into the Kingdom of God, into the mystery of Christianity, into an intimate relationship with Jesus Christ.

Yes, you have to pay a price. You have to be liberated. What you are liberated from varies from person to person. But liberation is necessary. Conversion is necessary. Repent! Then be baptised in the name of the Lord!

The majority of you here have, I suppose, been baptised. That was in the sacrament of Baptism—an extremely important moment. But we need, as I said before, to renew this, later, by means of a kind of fresh initiation. We need to choose for ourselves, accept, of our own free will, Jesus as Lord, Saviour, Redeemer.

We have to understand the full meaning of baptism. If I am unaware that I am a sinner, that I am weak, I cannot be aware that Jesus is my Saviour; I cannot be conscious that he is my Lord: by which I mean that he has the direction of my life.

Lord, what would you have me do? You are my Lord. My time, whether I be working or at leisure, is yours. You are my Lord. I ask you again, 'What would you have me do? What do you want of me today?'

Be open to the Holy Spirit

Yes, today. You have to make a choice, a decision as to your life. You have to ask: 'What is my vocation?' You cannot solve that problem alone. You have to ask the Lord: 'What would you have me do with my life? I have only one life. I want to make out of that life something of value, something for you. But what do you want of me?'

That is the question you must put. And then, having accepted Jesus as Redeemer, Saviour, Master, and Lord, be open to the Holy Spirit. Be assured you will receive the gift of the Holy Spirit.

Be open, then, to whatever the Holy Spirit will do. Be ready to let the Holy Spirit take over your life.

From time to time he will cause you a bit of trouble! The Holy Spirit does not always make things easy! On the morning of his coming at Pentecost there was something like an earthquake, you remember. You may have some surprises!

Be open to the Spirit, to his manifestations. I can promise you an adventure!

Bear in mind what the theologian Edward Schweizer says: 'Christians are expected not merely to possess the Spirit, but to possess it sensibly, tangibly. We wish to see it.'

When Paul came to one community he felt that, there, something was lacking..... 'Have you received the Spirit?' he asked. They said: 'No. What is the Spirit?' They had not even heard of the Spirit!

The first thing, then, we have to offer to the Holy Spirit for renewal is ourselves.

Renewal of communities

A second area will be renewal of Christian communities.

I am conscious—and glad to be made more conscious—that Oxford means colleges, communities. We are tempted to think of a university as a single entity. It is a good thing, therefore, to be reminded that it is made up of communities.

Similarly, in regard to the Church. We Catholics, in thinking about the Church, think usually of the universal Church.

We need to think, too, about the local Church. And not only the local Church as a community presided over by its bishop, but smaller and smaller communities.

Indeed, I think the future of Christianity will depend, to a large extent, on the renewal of our communities in their diversity. Whether these communities be large or small, the point is that we come together for the simple reason that we cannot be a Christian in isolation.

It has been said that to be intelligent, you need to be more than one—at least two or three. To be Christians, you have to be many. Plurality is essential. We pray in the plural. We act in the plural. I cannot love my neighbour unless some kind of a community exists.

In my book *A New Pentecost?* I began a chapter on this subject with two quotations which I think are invaluable.

One, that of Father Liégé, reads: 'Faith will be fraternal, that is, lived in community, or it will not exist at all.'

The second is that of Steve Clarke, one of the leaders of the 'Word of God' community of Ann Arbor Michigan, where there are hundreds of people living a Christian life together. 'What the Church needs,' it runs, 'more than new institutions or programs, are vital Christian communities.'

We need this independently of the social context of any particular time. It was needed from the beginning of the Church. It is needed now.

A challenge

But I would say that today there is another reason. To be a Christian today is a challenge. So much around us is non-Christian in atmosphere—even a negation of Christian values on every level, in every sphere.

If we turn on the television or radio, what we see and hear is, most of the time, far removed from Christianity. To remain critical, to remain oneself, to remain liberated, free, is very difficult.

We are more the sons of our times than of our parents. If we want to remain authentically what we are, we need to be part, in some way, of a community. We need, as it were, a buttress. We need this very strongly. That is why we should read again the Acts of the Apostles.

The early Church

In the second chapter of the Acts we have a description of the early Church: the first Christian community—our origin; our fountainhead. It is a well-known passage and one of deep significance.

88

Those first Christians met constantly, to share a common life, to hear the Apostles speak, to break bread, and to pray.

And what about ourselves, in our own communities? Sometimes we do not even know the name of the person next to us!

When Peter came out of prison the first thing he did was to go in search of a Christian community. And that is what we need, if we are to be true Christians: an apostolic community, a fraternal, Eucharistic, a prayerful community. We need community. We need this, if only to be able to listen together to the word of God.

We need it, also, to be in line with tradition— the living tradition that has been handed down to us. We need it, if we are to know whether our conversion is authentic: we need others to tell us—we will not discover this by ourselves. We cannot look at ourselves if we are alone.

A real community is a test, a support, a help: it liberates us from our inhibitions. It is a healing community. Once we belong to it, we feel that we complement each other.

The Church is indeed the body of Christ. And a body means complementarity of mind, hands, feet.

We need brothers and sisters. Athenagoras, Patriarch of Istanbul, speaking about the Pope, said: 'Even the Pope needs brothers.'

Visible and invisible

Renewal of self. Renewal of communities.
And, thirdly, renewal of the Church at large.
Here, a balance must be maintained between, on
the one hand the visible or institutional Church;
on the other hand, the invisible.

The Church cannot be only an institution or
society—not even if it were a perfect society. An
osmosis is necessary between visible and invisible, institutional and charismatic, the latter
instilling life into the former.

When I became a bishop in 1945 I chose for
my motto, to stress this need for osmosis and
chose for my motto, *'In Spiritu Sancto,'* 'In the
Holy Spirit.'

There can be tensions between the institutional and the charismatic. On the one
hand, Pope, bishops, hierarchy; on the other,
saints enkindled with the fire of the Spirit,
coming forward with courageous, challenging
enterprises.

I was aware of the duality. I read of it in the
pages of history; I encountered it in the
problems of some of my friends. My motto in-
spired me. I determined that whenever I felt that
breath of the Holy Spirit was blowing in a particular direction, as a bishop I would give what
help I could.

Without and with the Holy Spirit

For is not the Holy Spirit the life-principle of the Church? Let me quote from a text written by the Orthodox Bishop Ignatius and delivered at the Ecumenical Council of Churches at Uppsala in 1968, in which he draws a comparison between the Church with the Holy Spirit and the Church without the Holy Spirit:

> Without the Holy Spirit:
> God is far away;
> Christ stays in the past;
> The Gospel is a dead letter;
> The Church is an organisation;
> Authority is domination;
> Mission is propaganda;
> The liturgy no more than an evocation;
> Christian living, a slave morality.

With the Holy Spirit, the picture of the Church is a different one. By virtue of the Holy Spirit:

> The risen Christ is present;
> The Gospel is no longer a dead letter,
>   but the power of life;
> The Church is no longer merely an
>   organisation;
> It is communion with the Holy Trinity—
>   Father, Son, and Holy Spirit: this,
>   essentially, is what the Church means;

Authority is no longer domination:
  it is liberating service;
Mission is no longer propaganda;
The liturgy is memorial and anticipation;
Human action is divinised.

We see here how one facet of the Church complements another. The invisible needs to be supported by the visible, the spiritual by the institutional. Every form of revival must at some point find an institutional expression, if only to offer a guarantee of continuity.

Jean Monnet, one of the founders of Europe, says in his *Memoirs*—and his words are profound: *'Rien n'est possible sans les hommes, rien n'est durable sans les institutions.'* Nothing, he means, can be achieved unless there are those who will take the lead: equally nothing can last if there is no 'framework' to hold it together!

What about the spirit of St Francis of Assisi? Even that, whether we like it or not, has to be institutionalised to some degree, if the past is to be brought into the present, and the future ensured. It is something like sap in a tree. Only because the sap is enclosed in the trunk, and thus protected by the bark, can it in the fullness of time bring forth flowers and fruit.

The charismatic and the social-minded Christian
And this is the moment to say a word about

certain aspects of the Church which complement each other, and which, in view of the divisions among Christians today, are crucial.

There is a temptation, for example, to contrast the charismatic and the social-minded Christian, as if there were some kind of tension between those who put the emphasis on prayer, and others who could be described as social or politically orientated.

If you feel this tension it is best to realise, first of all, that there is no such thing as a non-charismatic Christian: every Christian is a charismatic, because every Christian is baptised in the Spirit. A non-charismatic Christian, therefore, does not exist. This is only logic.

Equally, the purely social Christian does not exist, because he is, by definition, rooted in Christianity. It is not a question of an 'either/or.' One complements the other.

To the charismatic-orientated Christian I would say: 'You are right in stressing the priority of grace and prayer.

It is important to react today against naturalism or activism. We cannot save the world unless we are closely united with God. We need, first of all, to be united with the Spirit.

If I am to speak here this evening aloud through the microphone, the electric power must be connected; otherwise nothing can be heard. The first thing is to put in the plug—the rest will follow.

Prayer, spirituality, the mystical life of the Church are essential: otherwise nothing happens. You are right to stress this. You need— every Christian needs— to enter the Upper Room.

The Upper Room

When the Lord left his Apostles, you remember, he said: 'Go to the Upper Room at Jerusalem and wait for me.' He did not say: 'Go rushing about the world!' No, he said: 'Wait!' Ten days of silence and prayer, with Mary, the holy women, and the others.

Wait! It is important that Christians should know that they have to await the coming of the Lord; they have to wait for grace, for the inspiration of the Holy Spirit.

But at the same time we must recognise the need to use all our human talents. We have not only to enter the Upper Room. We have to leave it, just as Peter left it on the morning of Pentecost, to bring the Gospel to every creature, to bring it in its full dimension to every person.

But even then, we are not totally aware of what Christianity means, what kind of person a Christian has to be.

Our catechisms usually tell us that we are created to know God, to love God, and to serve God. But this is not enough. It is only part of the answer. The full answer is: 'We are created to know God, to make him known; to love God, to make him loved; to serve God, and to make him served.' That is the answer in its full dimension.

Love translated into action

We cannot just absorb ourselves in spirituality without at the same time going out, as did the Apostles—participating on the social or the political level, as required. We have to go from the prayer meeting to the market place, from praying together to face the world together.

The gifts of the Spirit are not an end in themselves. They are meant to translate love into action. This is what I would say to the charismatic-minded Christian.

To the socially-minded Christian I would say: 'You are right in your positive views and statements. You are wrong in what you negate. You are right in stressing the needs of the world; the needs of the poor and the hungry. And you are right in stressing the unity between God and your neighbour. You cannot love God, and not love your neighbour: the bond goes too deep. Jesus is present in each of your neighbours: it is indeed important to stress this. But you are wrong if you forget our need of the Spirit to renew the face of the earth.'

We need his power and his gifts. We need the gift of prophecy to be able to speak bravely in

95

the world of today. When Dom Helder Camara says, rightly: 'This situation is unjust and inhuman,' he is using the gift of prophecy on the social level.

We need, too, on the social dimension, the gift of healing, because there are deep wounds in our structures.

We need the courage to believe that, in the power of the Spirit, we can work miracles. Yes, even that. Jesus said to us: 'I will not leave you alone. I will send you my Spirit. You will do greater things than I have done myself.' We have to believe this and to apply it in all the dimensions of human life.

We also need the Spirit to overcome the powers of darkness. I believe strongly in the reality of the powers of darkness. And, to renew the face of the earth, we need to be under the power of the Holy Spirit. In other words, the charismatic Christian stresses that God is living in him and with him; the social Christian, that the Lord is living in his neighbour, especially in the oppressed, in the socio-economic system of today.

The social Christian is tempted to speak about 'introverted Christianity' with a smile of superiority, claiming for himself "extroverted spirituality.' No, we must reject this dichotomy. Social concern must be rooted in faith.

The charismatic approach to social issues is

both initiated and carried out in the power of the Spirit. It is a matter not merely of theoretical principle, but of personal experience.

Our approach must be rooted in the essence of our Christianity if we want to be complete, balanced Christians. Charismatic and social go together. We have a double mission. The Lord said to the prophet Isaiah: 'The Lord will cause righteousness and praise to spring forth before all nations.' The Lord will cause righteousness and praise: both.

People are hungry

There is a fundamental spirit of faith and order in the Church as a whole. Christ did not come to establish a paradise on earth. 'My kingdom is not of this world.' The social concern of the Church and of Christians must not be confused with a temporal 'missionising' which regards the material welfare of mankind as the goal of all social activity.

In my book *The Gospel to Every Creature* I tried to make clear how much in error are those who believe that the full preaching of the Gospel of Jesus Christ should be postponed until men's lot has been improved by social action and they have accordingly been made receptive to the Gospel message. We have only to recall the Messianic words of Scripture: 'The poor will have the Gospel preached to them,' to realise

97

how fallacious is this heresy. The preaching of the Gospel must not be postponed.

I know, of course, that if a house is on fire, this is not the moment to preach! Our priority is to get water. But, this being said, it would be disastrous (yet this idea is going round)—to postpone the preaching of the Gospel until social conditions are better.

People are hungry for material aid—for bread. This is true. But they are also hungry for a reason to live. We have to provide both. The Christ who refuses to turn stones into bread, saying that man does not live by bread alone but by every word that comes out of the mouth of God, is the same Christ who feeds the multitude in the desert.

We are faced with a two-fold mission. We have to give the people bread and at the same time the sacred Host in the Eucharist. We have to teach them the alphabet and at the same time the catechism. We have to offer them social security and at the same time belief in the providence of God. We have to teach them the value of work and activity and at the same time the value of prayer. We have to save men's souls *and* their bodies.

We need at the same time social pioneers and saints. This is the only way to strike a balance: to overcome polarisation between opposing tendencies apparent in the Church today.

Facing the world

As Christians, we have to face the world. We have to be in the world, yet not immersed in it. It is a difficult situation.

Yes, we have to confront the world; and this means confronting imperialist oppression, economic domination, military might, religious conformism, state bureaucracy, and a continuous temptation to violence in support of causes, good as well as bad.

No spiritual renewal will have come of age until it has got to grips with this dimension of its responsibilities both to the Church and to the world.

I shall quote Mother Teresa of Calcutta who, in the United States, rightly spoke out about poverty. 'The greatest poverty,' she said, 'derives from your having a super-abundance of possessions. You lose that intimate touch with God. Spiritual poverty is much more difficult to relieve.'

Renewal of ourselves. Renewal of our communities. Renewal of our Church.

Towards visible unity

To end, I would like, in this ecumenical setting, to speak about the Holy Spirit as our guide towards visible unity among Christians.

We are living at an important moment in the history of the Church. An evolution is under way. I welcome the different statements originating from the Anglo-Roman Catholic International Commission (ARCIC): the Statements of Windsor, of Canterbury, and, more recently, of Venice. There is a move afoot, a process of clarification, a lifting of the fog. Even in London, I have discovered, the fog lifts!

Something indeed is happening. I believe in the work of reconciliation. I believe that the Holy Spirit is moving amongst us in his power and his strength—and moving quickly. I see great hope for the future if we are ready and willing to kneel down, together, in the presence of God.

Open to the Spirit

It is important there should be a continuance of dialogue between theologians, between the heads of Churches. But the fundamental dialogue to solve ecumenical problems and restore visible unity in the Church requires that all of us must be open to the breath of the Spirit, to the loving impatience of the Lord.

Moreover this dialogue will not be, essentially, one between, say, Rome and Canterbury, Rome and Moscow, Rome and Istanbul. No. The fundamental dialogue will take place between Rome and Jesus Christ, Canterbury and Jesus Christ, Moscow and Jesus Christ.

Together we shall have to come back to where

we started from. And this means coming back to the Upper Room in Jerusalem—that is, to the spirit of Pentecost.

'To arrive where we started'
You are familiar with the lines of T.S. Eliot—lines so rich in meaning:

'We shall not cease from exploration.
And the end of all our exploring
Will be to arrive where we started
And know the place for the first time.'

Let us, then, return home. We were born in the Upper Room. We were born there when the Lord, celebrating the Eucharist, set his seal upon the first Christian community. We were born there, again, at Pentecost.

Yes, it is to the Upper Room we must return.

Some years ago in Brussels, at a Congress of a thousand theologians at which I had to give the closing address, I was asked the question: 'How do you visualise the future? Now that we have had a First and a Second Vatican Council do you dream of seeing, one day, a Third Vatican Council?' 'No,' I answered, 'I don't think so. My dream is that we shall go, all together, to Jerusalem.'

A dream? Yes. But you know, perhaps, a Brazilian song which says that when one person alone dreams a dream, it is only a dream, but when two or more dream the same dream, this is the beginning of a reality.

Let us dream, together, of visible unity. Let us go, together, to Jerusalem.

To end, I would like to quote from the last interview given to a journalist by the late Athenagoras, Patriarch of the Orthodox Church, shortly before he died. He had, as you know, previously met Pope Paul.

'It was an important occasion,' he said, 'when my brother Paul and I embraced at the tomb of St Peter in Rome, and later in St Sophia's in Istanbul. It was an even more important occasion when my brother Paul and I embraced in Jerusalem—and there, found Jesus!'

The guidance of the Spirit

That is the future. I entrust it to your prayers, to your hopes. And I pray that we may, quite simply, follow the guidance of the Spirit.

Finally, a prayer from Cardinal Newman, and, also, a wish taken from St Paul's Epistle to the Ephesians.

Newman's prayer will be familiar to you:

'Lead, kindly Light, amid the encircling gloom,
Lead thou me on;

The night is dark, and I am far from home,
Lead thou me on.
Keep thou my feet; I do not ask to see
The distant scene; one step enough for me.'

And in St Paul's Epistle I find, condensed, all
that I have tried to say to you about the Father,
the Son, and the Holy Spirit. And this is my wish
to each one of you:

*'May the Holy Spirit fill you. Speak to one another in
psalms, hymns, and sacred songs.*
Sing and make music in your hearts to the Lord.
*And in the name of our Lord Jesus Christ give thanks
every day, for everything, to our God and Father.*
*'Glory be to the Father. Glory be to the Son. Glory be to
the Holy Spirit. Amen.'*